My Living Legacy

A Personal Journal to Guide Love Ones

This book is a gift for
my loved ones.

It contains memories
of a life well-lived.

Here, too, are my last wishes, requests,
hopes, dreams, gifts and good-byes
to my family and friends.

Library of Congress Cataloging-in-Publication Data

Fielder, Susan

    My Living Legacy: A Personal Journal to Guide Loved Ones.
      Susan Fielder

    ISBN 978-0692914823
    1. Death—Psychological aspects—Miscellanea.
    2. Autobiography—Authorship—Miscellanea.
    3. Estate planning—Miscellanea.

For information and ordering, contact:

info@MyLivingLegacy.life
www.MyLivingLegacy.life
email: susan@susanfielder.com

Available at Amazon: www.createspace.com/7347703

SUSAN
FIELDER
& ASSOCIATES, INC.
ideas that work!

Cover design by: Susan Fielder
Published by Susan Fielder & Associates, Inc.

Susan Fielder & Associates, Inc.
Printed in the United States of America
First Edition
The reader is to seek legal counsel regarding any legal issues or questions and topics that this book may cover. No part of this book should serve as a legal document, or as giving legal advice.

This book has been created with a great deal of care and thought to provide a place to record your life, personal feelings, memories, and wishes for the ultimate distribution of personal belongings.

This document is not binding and the user is urged to maintain a legal Will or Trust and consider the wishes contained herein as a personal supplement to guide your executor and heirs.

It is important to also create a **My Legacy Drawer** (See page 145) that can house the precious memories and important requests that you will address in this book. It will give you the peace of mind that you have organized your life as well as created a lasting memory for your loved ones. They will completely understand your wishes.

If you were to pass tomorrow,

*would your Will provide your family and friends
with all of the information they would want and need?
If not, imagine how their loss would be compounded
by having to make countless decisions without your
being there to counsel them.*

*This informal supplement to your legal **Will and Trust**
will help you organize and communicate to family and
loved ones your personal wishes, favorite memories,
and special feelings while preserving your legacy.*

Please take your time.

*This will become a treasure chest of life experiences.
Write in it as you would a journal or diary, making
changes as needed. Embellish it with articles and pictures.
Whatever you make of it, it will be cherished
in the hearts of those you leave behind.*

That's a promise!

"Keep a journal of your dreams,
goals and accomplishments.
If your life is worth living,
it's worth recording."

— Marilyn Grey

Contents

4. The Long Road Home

5. Exit Dancing

6. Practical Issues

7. Sands of Time

"If we all discovered that we had only five minutes left to say all that we wanted to say, every cellphone would be occupied by people calling other people to tell them that they loved them."

— *Christopher Morley*

Foreward

I came upon this project out of pain and grief, but mostly out of necessity. While everyone is eager for the celebration surrounding the birth of a new life, it is with trepidation and procrastination we prepare for our passing. Tomorrow seems a perfect choice for dispersing what has taken a lifetime to accumulate. My mother had planned on living forever, it seemed, and then a wild card took us by surprise, and in a matter of weeks she was gone. In a bedroom drawer I discovered a simpler version of this book, one that I had given her three years earlier. The pages were a blank, pristine white, like clean sheets on a freshly made bed, unmarred by a restless sleeper. It lay empty, much like our bodies do without a spirit. I could only imagine what secrets had never been written, what wishes had never been shared.

Truly you cannot judge a book by its cover, for a book is nothing at all without its contents. I was left in the wake of my mother's leaving to struggle with my brothers over details and deadlines, caught between fairness and futility. Nothing in this world truly belongs to us; rather we are entrusted as caretakers, shepherds in the field of life. My hope is that the anguish of others will be diminished through the use of this journal. So, I encourage you to take the time to fill this out, while the sun is still high in the sky, and leave a legacy to comfort your loved ones in the days and weeks after your death. On these pages you can provide answers to the many questions that remain once you are gone.

— Susan Fielder

PRINT YOUR NAME BELOW

My Wishes

Within this book, I have gathered my special thoughts, memories, and requests, which I am leaving for my family and friends. It contains personal recollections, feelings about my life, and my requests for distribution of certain belongings.

I recognize that this is not a legal supplement of my Will or Trust; however, any requests herein are expressed in good faith to my Executor in the hope that they will be honored. Above all, I trust that my loved ones will enjoy this personal perspective of my life and be assured of my fondest farewell wishes. I have created **My Legacy Drawer** (Page 145) that will make it easier to find all documents.

Signed _____

        on this _____ day of _____ in the year _____

I entrust this book to _____

Relationship _____

Address _____

Phone _____ Cell _____

email _____

Notes _____

_____

_____

In the event this guardian is someone other than my Executor, I hope that my Executor will honor my wishes to utilize the person named above as my chosen spokesperson for the requests outlined herein. In case the above person is not able to carry out my wishes at the time of my death,

I choose _____ as an alternate.

Relationship _____

Address _____

Phone _____ Cell _____

email _____

Notes _____

_____

_____

"True wealth is not measured in money
or status or power. It is measured in the
legacy we leave behind for those we love."

— *César Chávez*

Chapter 1

The Tapestry of Life
Experiences That Shaped My Destiny

Our lives are finely woven and richly textured, echoing the events and relationships that cross our paths. Prized trophies, framed diplomas, baby shoes, and wedding albums—these are reminders of the experiences that shaped our destiny. What was once an obstacle becomes a stepping stone. Many times we choose to participate, but ultimately our destiny is held in the hands of the Master Sculptor as our lives are invisibly shaped. Whether by accident or divine appointment, we arrive at places we never could have dreamed, endured hardships we never could have imagined, and come out on the other side of the storm a better person. For some life is navigated with precision, while others drive kamikaze-style into the night with empty pockets and a tank full of dreams, willing to go wherever the road leads. With inspired direction or reckless abandon, we run after the magic of living, its fine nuances and subtle opportunities rising and falling into a crescendo of possibility. These golden threads highlight our existence in the tapestry called life, forever changing their lyrical pattern as lives intertwine.

An individual's life

becomes intricately sculpted over time

through an accumulation of diverse elements: guiding

philosophies, seemingly insignificant incidents, enjoyable

pastimes or hobbies, favorite foods, adventuresome

travels, and beloved poems, books, and music. Many times

the circumstances that shape our lives are unknown or

eventually forgotten by others.

The following pages prompt you to record those things

that move you, bring a smile to your face, or encourage

you through one of life's storms. You may wish to attach

newspaper articles, recipes, pictures, printed poems, or

other items to which you often refer.

Your Achievements

"Life is no brief candle to me. It is a sort of splendid torch which I have got a hold of for the moment, and I want to make it burn as brightly as possible before handing it on to future generations."

— *George Bernard Shaw*

Memorable
Moments

Everybody has them. You know what yours are. Leave them behind for others to learn more about you – to be surprised and delighted.

Life-Changing Events

Was it fate, planned, or chance? Whether they were hard work or good fortune, share the experiences that shifted your destiny.

Inspirational Thoughts, Guiding Words of Advice & Wisdom

Record the famous last words, notable quotes, or philosophies that steered your life's course.

_____

_____

_____

_____

_____

_____

_____

_____

_____

_____

_____

_____

_____

_____

_____

_____

_____

_____

_____

_____

_____

The Faith Factor

*Share your spiritual
experiences and beliefs.*

It Was So Romantic

A starry night, a stolen kiss—please tell us now, it was such bliss!

_____

_____

_____

_____

_____

_____

_____

_____

_____

_____

_____

_____

_____

_____

_____

_____

_____

_____

Secrets

You promised you'd never tell . . . well, here's your chance!

Great Adventures

What exciting escapades can you share? Do tell.

Favorite Travels

*Pack a bag, get a map!
Tell where you've been
and who you've met.*

*List the cities, countries
and all that you've seen.
And, don't forget the
stories in between.*

Small-World Stories

Around the block, across the country, or halfway around the globe, chance meetings make it a small world.

Favorite Books, Movies & Plays

Encore! Encore! Whether you read it, watched it, or applauded it, share your favorites and the reasons why.

_____

_____

_____

_____

_____

_____

_____

_____

_____

_____

_____

_____

_____

_____

_____

_____

_____

_____

_____

Poems & Quotes

"Live your life so that your children can tell their children that you not only stood for something wonderful . . . you acted on it."

— *Dan Zadra*

_____

_____

_____

_____

_____

_____

_____

_____

_____

_____

_____

_____

_____

_____

_____

_____

_____

_____

_____

Recipes I Made Famous

Recipe for Eating Crow

Buy one extra large crow, making sure it is tough and difficult to swallow. Marinate overnight with remorse. Sprinkle generously with sincere apologies and bake at a high temperature. Stew frequently in your own juices until very uncomfortable. Serve quickly and garnish with a fresh request for forgiveness.

Now, add your real recipes!

Drawings

A picture is worth a thousand words. Tape them here, or tell us where they are!

Chase your dreams and follow your art!

Paste in, color it, but be sure you start!

You can listen to music as you must,

But don't let this page collect any dust!

– Susan Fielder

Games & Hobbies

Win or lose, it's how you played! Name your game, collectible, or favorite pastime.

Playing guitar, Mexican trains, Canasta and learning new things on TED® talks. Searching Google's Cultural Arts site is the best!

My Life Story

*This is your opportunity
to share your own story.
No one can tell it like you.*

Add your résumé here.

What's on your bucket list Top 10?

- *Visit all 50 States*
- *Visit Portugal*
- *See the Gaudí Buildings in Barcelona*
- *Pay it forward by buying someone's lunch*
- *Walk the Great Wall of China*
- *Spend a night in a tree house*
- *Change someone's life*
- *Learn how to paint*
- *Learn a language*

Your single most life-changing event

Share a decision that changed your destiny.

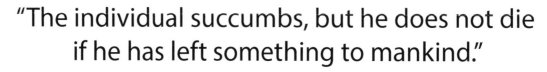

"The individual succumbs, but he does not die
if he has left something to mankind."

— *Will Durant*

When I Couldn't Find the Words

Special Notes to and About Others

In the electronic age of computers, iPads, television, video games, and voice mail, the written word has taken a backseat to the ease of texting, calling on your smart phone or the light taps of a keyboard to share your thoughts. But often we leave the most important things unsaid, swept away in an ocean of mundane day-to-day activities. These private memories will live on long after we are gone, to comfort our loved ones in tangible ways, to be read and remembered. More important than leaving behind financial security and belongings is leaving behind your spirit, your voice, your connection to others, a bridge that can touch the living in the gap left behind after death.

When I Couldn't Find the Words

Imagine for a moment

the conversation you would want to share with a loved one, knowing that you had only a few hours left together, and simply begin writing down or recording on your smart phone. You may convey your message in letter form, capture it on a tape recorder, camcorder, DVD, or smart phone or treat it as a diary passage, dating each entry as you record it. If any unresolved issues linger in your personal relationships, now is the time to put them to rest. We all have special people who have influenced the course of our life and helped create who we are. It is nice to acknowledge them in a letter or even a call to tell them what they mean to you.

Below is a list so you can add names of those kind folks in which you would like to say special words:

Spouse	Other family members:	Friends
Children	Nieces	Teachers
Stepchildren	Nephews	Religious leaders,
Siblings	Cousins	Mentors
Parents	In-laws	Charities
Grandparents	Aunts	and more.
	Uncles	

"With the best that was in me
I have tried to write more happiness
into the world."

— *Last words of Frances Burnett*

The following pages are designed to be cut and removed from the book. This is so you can write a private note to someone special.

Once you have completed the page, cut along the dotted line and then fold into thirds as shown.
Place in an envelope and add it to **My Legacy Drawer** (See page 145) under a *Personal Letters Folder.*

A Special Note To

_____

_____

_____

_____

_____

_____

_____

_____

_____

_____

_____

_____

_____

_____

_____

_____

_____

_____

_____

_____

A Special Note To:

A Special Note To:

FOLD LINE

A Special Note To:

FOLD LINE

A Special Note To:

FOLD LINE

A Special Note To:

FOLD LINE

A Special Note To

_____

_____

_____

_____

_____

_____

_____

_____

_____

_____

_____

_____

_____

_____

_____

_____

_____

_____

_____

YOU MAY CUT AND REMOVE THIS PAGE TO SEND THIS SPECIAL NOTE

A Special Note To

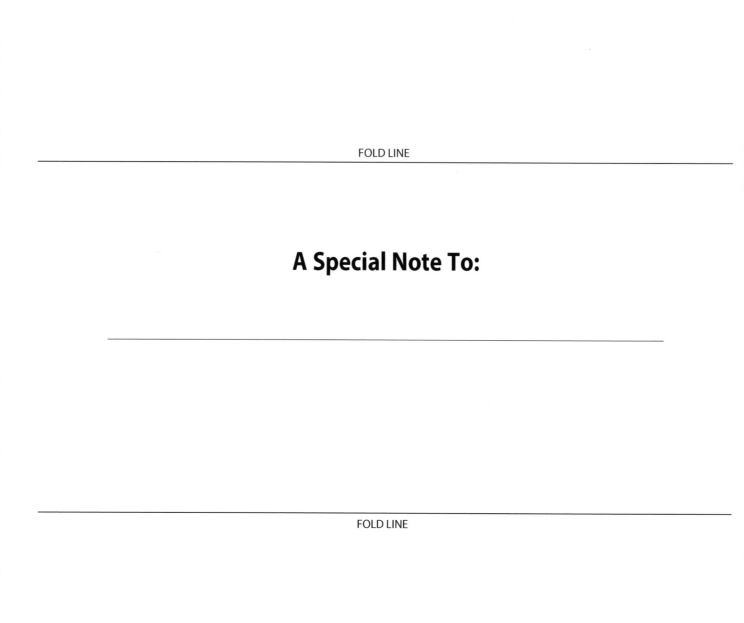

FOLD LINE

A Special Note To:

FOLD LINE

A Special Note To:

YOU MAY CUT AND REMOVE THIS PAGE TO SEND THIS SPECIAL NOTE

_____

_____

_____

_____

_____

_____

_____

_____

_____

_____

_____

_____

_____

_____

_____

_____

_____

_____

FOLD LINE

A Special Note To:

_____

FOLD LINE

A Special Note To:

_____

_____

_____

_____

_____

_____

_____

_____

_____

_____

_____

_____

_____

_____

_____

_____

_____

_____

_____

_____

YOU MAY CUT AND REMOVE THIS PAGE TO SEND THIS SPECIAL NOTE

FOLD LINE

A Special Note To:

FOLD LINE

A Special Note To:

_____

_____

_____

_____

_____

_____

_____

_____

_____

_____

_____

_____

_____

_____

_____

_____

_____

_____

_____

_____

YOU MAY CUT AND REMOVE THIS PAGE TO SEND THIS SPECIAL NOTE

A Special Note To:

A Special Note To:

YOU MAY CUT AND REMOVE THIS PAGE TO SEND THIS SPECIAL NOTE

_____

_____

_____

_____

_____

_____

_____

_____

_____

_____

_____

_____

_____

_____

_____

_____

_____

_____

_____

_____

FOLD LINE

A Special Note To:

FOLD LINE

A Special Note To:

_____

_____

_____

_____

_____

_____

_____

_____

_____

_____

_____

_____

_____

_____

_____

_____

_____

_____

YOU MAY CUT AND REMOVE THIS PAGE TO SEND THIS SPECIAL NOTE

A Special Note To:

A Special Note To:

_____

_____

_____

_____

_____

_____

_____

_____

_____

_____

_____

_____

_____

_____

_____

_____

_____

_____

_____

_____

YOU MAY CUT AND REMOVE THIS PAGE TO SEND THIS SPECIAL NOTE

FOLD LINE

A Special Note To:

FOLD LINE

A Special Note To:

_____

_____

_____

_____

_____

_____

_____

_____

_____

_____

_____

_____

_____

_____

_____

_____

_____

_____

_____

_____

_____

YOU MAY CUT AND REMOVE THIS PAGE TO SEND THIS SPECIAL NOTE

"Love is the only thing we can carry
with us when we go, and it makes
the end so easy."

— *Louisa May Alcott*

Chapter 3

You Can't Take it with You
Distribution of My Worldly Possessions

I know a woman who has what she calls the "handbag theory" of life. It's a simple one, she claims, because we have a tendency to complicate things that would happen naturally. Her theory is this: no matter how large or how small a purse you carry, it always ends up full—with enough room for what you need to get by, and then some. And while it's true a larger handbag will hold more things, many times they are difficult to find. Now with a smaller purse, you've got less to look after, and it's a whole lot easier to carry. The same holds true for living. It seems ironic that we leave this world about the same as when we came in, hopefully no worse for the wear, only we have accumulated some stuff along the way. So, whether you have a lot or a little, she says, choose carefully what you do with it, and divine providence will take care of the rest. Because, after all, you can't take it with you; you can only enjoy it while you're here.

What you decide here

regarding your possessions and their distribution

can help keep peace within your family and preserve your keepsakes in a very special and thoughtful way. The fill-in-the-blank format allows you to date and change entries whenever you wish.

Even close families can succumb to hurt feelings, misunderstandings, or estrangement when it comes time to distribute personal belongings. The "It won't matter when I'm gone" mindset is a bitter legacy to leave your loved ones, especially if they were promised something in confidence before your death. Remember, though, it is necessary that distributions abide by the legal process as directed by your executor.

Below is a list to guide you in cataloging your possessions. Choose the appropriate categories and itemize on the following pages. With digital cameras and smart phones, it is easy to take a photo and place a copy of the item next to the name of the recipient.

Vehicles	*Books*	*Smartphones*
Artwork	*Diaries/Letters/Writings*	*China*
Jewelry	*Photo Albums*	*Silver*
Furniture	*Scrapbooks*	*Crystal*
Small Appliances	*Antique Collectibles*	*Linens*
Computers/Tablets	*Musical Instruments*	*Clothing*
Electronics/Cameras	*Sports Equipment*	*Holiday Decorations*
Music/Videos	*Tools*	*Others*

Remember Me by These Special Things

Time to make a List of Special Things and to whom you would like to gift.

Make a list below and check off as you have completed the form for each of these gifts.*

Name   Gift

☐ _____   _____

☐ _____   _____

☐ _____   _____

☐ _____   _____

☐ _____   _____

☐ _____   _____

☐ _____   _____

☐ _____   _____

☐ _____   _____

☐ _____   _____

☐ _____   _____

☐ _____   _____

☐ _____   _____

☐ _____   _____

☐ _____   _____

☐ _____   _____

☐ _____   _____

☐ _____   _____

*Note: Photocopy this page for additional room for names and gifts.

Remember Me by These Special Things

*My wishes are for the distribution of my personal belongings as follows.
At the time of my death, if any item is not in my estate, then the gifts shall lapse.
If any beneficiary has passed away, then the gifts shall be either distributed in
accordance with the terms of my Will or discretion of my Executor.*

_____
(Category)

Item(s) _____ Date _____

Description and/or History_____

_____

Location _____

Is Bequeathed to_____

Phone _____ Cell _____

email _____

_____
(Category)

Item(s) _____ Date _____

Description and/or History_____

_____

Location _____

Is Bequeathed to_____

Phone _____ Cell _____

email _____

(Category) _____

Item(s) _____ Date _____

Description and/or History_____

_____

Location _____

Is Bequeathed to_____

Phone _____ Cell _____

email _____

(Category) _____

Item(s) _____ Date _____

Description and/or History_____

_____

Location _____

Is Bequeathed to_____

Phone _____ Cell _____

email _____

(Category) _____

Item(s) _____ Date _____

Description and/or History_____

_____

Location _____

Is Bequeathed to_____

Phone _____ Cell _____

email _____

_____
(Category)

Item(s) _____ Date _____

Description and/or History_____

_____

Location _____

Is Bequeathed to_____

Phone _____ Cell _____

email _____

_____
(Category)

Item(s) _____ Date _____

Description and/or History_____

_____

Location _____

Is Bequeathed to_____

Phone _____ Cell _____

email _____

_____
(Category)

Item(s) _____ Date _____

Description and/or History_____

_____

Location _____

Is Bequeathed to_____

Phone _____ Cell _____

email _____

(Category) _____

Item(s) _____ Date _____

Description and/or History _____

_____

Location _____

Is Bequeathed to _____

Phone _____ Cell _____

email _____

(Category) _____

Item(s) _____ Date _____

Description and/or History _____

_____

Location _____

Is Bequeathed to _____

Phone _____ Cell _____

email _____

(Category) _____

Item(s) _____ Date _____

Description and/or History _____

_____

Location _____

Is Bequeathed to _____

Phone _____ Cell _____

email _____

_____
(Category)

Item(s) _____ Date _____

Description and/or History_____

_____

Location _____

Is Bequeathed to_____

Phone _____ Cell _____

email _____

_____
(Category)

Item(s) _____ Date _____

Description and/or History_____

_____

Location _____

Is Bequeathed to_____

Phone _____ Cell _____

email _____

_____
(Category)

Item(s) _____ Date _____

Description and/or History_____

_____

Location _____

Is Bequeathed to_____

Phone _____ Cell _____

email _____

_____
(Category)

Item(s) _____ Date _____

Description and/or History_____

_____

Location _____

Is Bequeathed to_____

Phone _____ Cell _____

email _____

_____
(Category)

Item(s) _____ Date _____

Description and/or History_____

_____

Location _____

Is Bequeathed to_____

Phone _____ Cell _____

email _____

_____
(Category)

Item(s) _____ Date _____

Description and/or History_____

_____

Location _____

Is Bequeathed to_____

Phone _____ Cell _____

email _____

_____
(Category)

Item(s) _____ Date _____

Description and/or History_____

_____

Location _____

Is Bequeathed to_____

Phone _____ Cell _____

email _____

_____
(Category)

Item(s) _____ Date _____

Description and/or History_____

_____

Location _____

Is Bequeathed to_____

Phone _____ Cell _____

email _____

_____
(Category)

Item(s) _____ Date _____

Description and/or History_____

_____

Location _____

Is Bequeathed to_____

Phone _____ Cell _____

email _____

(Category) _____

Item(s) _____ Date _____

Description and/or History _____

_____

Location _____

Is Bequeathed to _____

Phone _____ Cell _____

email _____

(Category) _____

Item(s) _____ Date _____

Description and/or History _____

_____

Location _____

Is Bequeathed to _____

Phone _____ Cell _____

email _____

(Category) _____

Item(s) _____ Date _____

Description and/or History _____

_____

Location _____

Is Bequeathed to _____

Phone _____ Cell _____

email _____

(Category) _____

Item(s) _____ Date _____

Description and/or History_____

_____

Location _____

Is Bequeathed to_____

Phone _____ Cell _____

email _____

(Category) _____

Item(s) _____ Date _____

Description and/or History_____

_____

Location _____

Is Bequeathed to_____

Phone _____ Cell _____

email _____

(Category) _____

Item(s) _____ Date _____

Description and/or History_____

_____

Location _____

Is Bequeathed to_____

Phone _____ Cell _____

email _____

(Category) _____

Item(s) _____ Date _____

Description and/or History _____

_____

Location _____

Is Bequeathed to _____

Phone _____ Cell _____

email _____

(Category) _____

Item(s) _____ Date _____

Description and/or History _____

_____

Location _____

Is Bequeathed to _____

Phone _____ Cell _____

email _____

(Category) _____

Item(s) _____ Date _____

Description and/or History _____

_____

Location _____

Is Bequeathed to _____

Phone _____ Cell _____

email _____

(Category)

Item(s) _____ Date _____

Description and/or History _____

_____

Location _____

Is Bequeathed to _____

Phone _____ Cell _____

email _____

(Category)

Item(s) _____ Date _____

Description and/or History _____

_____

Location _____

Is Bequeathed to _____

Phone _____ Cell _____

email _____

(Category)

Item(s) _____ Date _____

Description and/or History _____

_____

Location _____

Is Bequeathed to _____

Phone _____ Cell _____

email _____

(Category)

Item(s) _____ Date _____

Description and/or History _____

_____

Location _____

Is Bequeathed to _____

Phone _____ Cell _____

email _____

(Category)

Item(s) _____ Date _____

Description and/or History _____

_____

Location _____

Is Bequeathed to _____

Phone _____ Cell _____

email _____

(Category)

Item(s) _____ Date _____

Description and/or History _____

_____

Location _____

Is Bequeathed to _____

Phone _____ Cell _____

email _____

_____
(Category)

Item(s) _____ Date _____

Description and/or History_____

_____

Location _____

Is Bequeathed to_____

Phone _____ Cell _____

email _____

_____
(Category)

Item(s) _____ Date _____

Description and/or History_____

_____

Location _____

Is Bequeathed to_____

Phone _____ Cell _____

email _____

_____
(Category)

Item(s) _____ Date _____

Description and/or History_____

_____

Location _____

Is Bequeathed to_____

Phone _____ Cell _____

email _____

(Category)

Item(s) _____ Date _____

Description and/or History _____

_____

Location _____

Is Bequeathed to _____

Phone _____ Cell _____

email _____

(Category)

Item(s) _____ Date _____

Description and/or History _____

_____

Location _____

Is Bequeathed to _____

Phone _____ Cell _____

email _____

(Category)

Item(s) _____ Date _____

Description and/or History _____

_____

Location _____

Is Bequeathed to _____

Phone _____ Cell _____

email _____

_____
(Category)

Item(s) _____ Date _____

Description and/or History_____

_____

Location _____

Is Bequeathed to_____

Phone _____ Cell _____

email _____

_____
(Category)

Item(s) _____ Date _____

Description and/or History_____

_____

Location _____

Is Bequeathed to_____

Phone _____ Cell _____

email _____

_____
(Category)

Item(s) _____ Date _____

Description and/or History_____

_____

Location _____

Is Bequeathed to_____

Phone _____ Cell _____

email _____

(Category) _____

Item(s) _____ Date _____

Description and/or History_____

_____

Location _____

Is Bequeathed to_____

Phone _____ Cell _____

email _____

(Category) _____

Item(s) _____ Date _____

Description and/or History_____

_____

Location _____

Is Bequeathed to_____

Phone _____ Cell _____

email _____

(Category) _____

Item(s) _____ Date _____

Description and/or History_____

_____

Location _____

Is Bequeathed to_____

Phone _____ Cell _____

email _____

_____
(Category)

Item(s) _____ Date _____

Description and/or History_____

_____

Location _____

Is Bequeathed to_____

Phone _____ Cell _____

email _____

_____
(Category)

Item(s) _____ Date _____

Description and/or History_____

_____

Location _____

Is Bequeathed to_____

Phone _____ Cell _____

email _____

_____
(Category)

Item(s) _____ Date _____

Description and/or History_____

_____

Location _____

Is Bequeathed to_____

Phone _____ Cell _____

email _____

_____
(Category)

Item(s) _____ Date _____

Description and/or History_____

_____

Location _____

Is Bequeathed to_____

Phone _____ Cell _____

email _____

_____
(Category)

Item(s) _____ Date _____

Description and/or History_____

_____

Location _____

Is Bequeathed to_____

Phone _____ Cell _____

email _____

_____
(Category)

Item(s) _____ Date _____

Description and/or History_____

_____

Location _____

Is Bequeathed to_____

Phone _____ Cell _____

email _____

(Category)

Item(s) _____ Date _____

Description and/or History_____

_____

Location _____

Is Bequeathed to_____

Phone _____ Cell _____

email _____

(Category)

Item(s) _____ Date _____

Description and/or History_____

_____

Location _____

Is Bequeathed to_____

Phone _____ Cell _____

email _____

(Category)

Item(s) _____ Date _____

Description and/or History_____

_____

Location _____

Is Bequeathed to_____

Phone _____ Cell _____

email _____

(Category) _____

Item(s) _____ Date _____

Description and/or History_____

_____

Location _____

Is Bequeathed to_____

Phone _____ Cell _____

email _____

(Category) _____

Item(s) _____ Date _____

Description and/or History_____

_____

Location _____

Is Bequeathed to_____

Phone _____ Cell _____

email _____

(Category) _____

Item(s) _____ Date _____

Description and/or History_____

_____

Location _____

Is Bequeathed to_____

Phone _____ Cell _____

email _____

_____
(Category)

Item(s) _____ Date _____

Description and/or History_____

_____

Location _____

Is Bequeathed to_____

Phone _____ Cell _____

email _____

_____
(Category)

Item(s) _____ Date _____

Description and/or History_____

_____

Location _____

Is Bequeathed to_____

Phone _____ Cell _____

email _____

_____
(Category)

Item(s) _____ Date _____

Description and/or History_____

_____

Location _____

Is Bequeathed to_____

Phone _____ Cell _____

email _____

(Category) _____

Item(s) _____ Date _____

Description and/or History_____

_____

Location _____

Is Bequeathed to_____

Phone _____ Cell _____

email _____

(Category) _____

Item(s) _____ Date _____

Description and/or History_____

_____

Location _____

Is Bequeathed to_____

Phone _____ Cell _____

email _____

(Category) _____

Item(s) _____ Date _____

Description and/or History_____

_____

Location _____

Is Bequeathed to_____

Phone _____ Cell _____

email _____

_____
(Category)

Item(s) _____ Date _____

Description and/or History_____

_____

Location _____

Is Bequeathed to_____

Phone _____ Cell _____

email _____

_____
(Category)

Item(s) _____ Date _____

Description and/or History_____

_____

Location _____

Is Bequeathed to_____

Phone _____ Cell _____

email _____

_____
(Category)

Item(s) _____ Date _____

Description and/or History_____

_____

Location _____

Is Bequeathed to_____

Phone _____ Cell _____

email _____

(Category) _____

Item(s) _____ Date _____

Description and/or History_____

_____

Location _____

Is Bequeathed to_____

Phone _____ Cell _____

email _____

(Category) _____

Item(s) _____ Date _____

Description and/or History_____

_____

Location _____

Is Bequeathed to_____

Phone _____ Cell _____

email _____

(Category) _____

Item(s) _____ Date _____

Description and/or History_____

_____

Location _____

Is Bequeathed to_____

Phone _____ Cell _____

email _____

_____
(Category)

Item(s) _____ Date _____

Description and/or History_____

_____

Location _____

Is Bequeathed to_____

Phone _____ Cell _____

email _____

_____
(Category)

Item(s) _____ Date _____

Description and/or History_____

_____

Location _____

Is Bequeathed to_____

Phone _____ Cell _____

email _____

_____
(Category)

Item(s) _____ Date _____

Description and/or History_____

_____

Location _____

Is Bequeathed to_____

Phone _____ Cell _____

email _____

My Pet & Loyal Companion

Pet's Name _____ Birthday _____

    Nicknames_____

Breed _____ Registration Numbers _____

Identifying Marks _____

My Pet's Likes and Dislikes _____

Favorite Toys _____

Favorite Scratch Spot _____

Foods _____

Habits_____

Tricks_____

Medical History _____

Veterinarian _____

    Phone _____

Daycare_____

    Phone _____

I would like to leave _____

    In the care of _____

    Phone _____

If my selected caretaker is unable to fulfill my wish, my preferred alternates listed in

order are as follows: *(Make sure designated person is aware of this responsibility.)*

_____

_____

_____

*(Keep more detailed information about your pet in **My Legacy Drawer.** See page 145)*

My Pet & Loyal Companion

Pet's Name _____ Birthday _____

    Nicknames _____

Breed _____ Registration Numbers _____

Identifying Marks _____

My Pet's Likes and Dislikes _____

Favorite Toys _____

Favorite Scratch Spot _____

Foods _____

Habits _____

Tricks _____

Medical History _____

Veterinarian _____

    Phone _____

Daycare _____

    Phone _____

I would like to leave _____

    In the care of _____

    Phone _____

If my selected caretaker is unable to fulfill my wish, my preferred alternates listed in

order are as follows: *(Make sure designated person is aware of this responsibility.)*

_____

_____

_____

_____

*(Keep more detailed information about your pet in **My Legacy Drawer**. See page 145)*

Sentimental Drawer – Notes and Thoughts

Each of us has sentimental thoughts and items. We keep them in many places — journals, scraps of paper, 3" x 5" cards, shoe boxes, drawers, and more.

*This is a place to keep them. Or, you can add a folder to **My Legacy Drawer** and keep them there or keep larger objects in **My Sentimental Drawer.***

_____

_____

_____

_____

_____

_____

_____

_____

_____

_____

_____

_____

_____

_____

_____

_____

Location of My Sentimental Drawer: _____

_____

Personal Notes

"A long life may not be good enough,
but a good life is long enough."

— *Benjamin Franklin*

Chapter 4

The Long Road Home
My Family History

Photo albums rest in a pile, stacked and strewn haphazardly. These albums are my family and friends, my heritage, my past. Inside, though the pages are yellow and tattered, the images spring to life like the warm glow radiating from a winter fire. These memories give me pleasure, conjuring up the smell of warm pies, sweet lullabies, and wishes made on shooting stars. I remember the soft skin of my grandmother as she cradled me in her arms, a pillow of love on which I lay my head. I slept in the same bed my mother slept in as a girl, and her mother before her. I close my eyes and surround myself with the cool dank of the attic in summer, a secret hideaway of long forgotten dances and diaries, desires and disappointments, remnants of a yesterday I yearn to experience again. I feel connected, part of the universal scheme, a descendant of and an heir to the rich history of my ancestors. To anyone else, these photos are nameless faces, but to me they are my lifeblood, coursing the long road home through each generation.

While few people have the time

or interest to become genealogists,
you can preserve priceless segments of family history that
might otherwise be lost forever. Here you are encouraged to
capture unique, inspiring, or touching family stories that
impart valuable life lessons.

It is essential that you begin recording whatever information you do have, however sketchy or incomplete it might be. Begin with your family tree, and follow by documenting useful information about family medical history and any hereditary conditions. Even one entry will expand your relatives' appreciation and understanding of their ancestral origins.

To provide an added touch, you may wish to record family heritage by interviewing relatives on electronic devices. You may even interview yourself. Many times this can help loved ones through the grieving process.

Be sure to record the locations of all tapes, videos, CDs, DVDs, movies made and all backups from computers in the appropriate journal section so that they can be found in **My Legacy Drawer** *(See page 145). All precious items from the past should be included. You may also want create a* **My Sentimental Drawer** *(See page 98).*

Historical Family Stories That are Folklore

Tell us now about the colorful folks you call family, where they came from and what they did. The following pages are for you to record stories from family history involving parents, grandparents, siblings, or any other family member. Enter things as you would in a diary, adding bits here and there, and don't worry about the sequence or form.

Your Immediate Family Tree

YOUR NAME

SPOUSE

BORN _____ DIED _____ MARRIED _____ BORN _____ DIED _____

CHILD #1

SPOUSE

BORN _____ DIED _____ MARRIED _____ BORN _____ DIED _____

GRANDCHILD #1

GRANDCHILD #2

GRANDCHILD #3

BORN _____ DIED _____ BORN _____ DIED _____ BORN _____ DIED _____

CHILD #2

SPOUSE

BORN _____ DIED _____ MARRIED _____ BORN _____ DIED _____

GRANDCHILD #1

GRANDCHILD #2

GRANDCHILD #3

BORN _____ DIED _____ BORN _____ DIED _____ BORN _____ DIED _____

CHILD #3

SPOUSE

BORN _____ DIED _____ MARRIED _____ BORN _____ DIED _____

GRANDCHILD #1

GRANDCHILD #2

GRANDCHILD #3

BORN _____ DIED _____ BORN _____ DIED _____ BORN _____ DIED _____

CHILD #4

SPOUSE

BORN _____ DIED _____ MARRIED _____ BORN _____ DIED _____

GRANDCHILD #1

GRANDCHILD #2

GRANDCHILD #3

BORN _____ DIED _____ BORN _____ DIED _____ BORN _____ DIED _____

Your Extended Family Tree

NAME

Name

BORN _____ DIED _____ MARRIED_____ BORN _____ DIED _____

STEPCHILD #1

SPOUSE

BORN _____ DIED _____ MARRIED_____ BORN _____ DIED _____

GRANDCHILD #1   **GRANDCHILD #2**   **GRANDCHILD #3**

BORN _____ DIED _____ BORN _____ DIED _____ BORN _____ DIED _____

STEPCHILD #2

SPOUSE

BORN _____ DIED _____ MARRIED_____ BORN _____ DIED _____

GRANDCHILD #1   **GRANDCHILD #2**   **GRANDCHILD #3**

BORN _____ DIED _____ BORN _____ DIED _____ BORN _____ DIED _____

STEPCHILD #3

SPOUSE

BORN _____ DIED _____ MARRIED_____ BORN _____ DIED _____

GRANDCHILD #1   **GRANDCHILD #2**   **GRANDCHILD #3**

BORN _____ DIED _____ BORN _____ DIED _____ BORN _____ DIED _____

STEPCHILD #4

SPOUSE

BORN _____ DIED _____ MARRIED_____ BORN _____ DIED _____

GRANDCHILD #1   **GRANDCHILD #2**   **GRANDCHILD #3**

BORN _____ DIED _____ BORN _____ DIED _____ BORN _____ DIED _____

Your Ancestors' Family Tree

GRANDFATHER

GRANDMOTHER

GRANDFATHER

GRANDMOTHER

MARRIED_____

MARRIED_____

BORN _____ DIED _____ BORN _____ DIED _____ BORN _____ DIED _____ BORN _____ DIED _____

FATHER

BORN _____ DIED _____

SIBLING

BORN _____ DIED _____

SIBLING

BORN _____ DIED _____

SIBLING

BORN _____ DIED _____

MOTHER

BORN _____ DIED _____

SIBLING

BORN _____ DIED _____

SIBLING

BORN _____ DIED _____

SIBLING

BORN _____ DIED _____

YOUR NAME

BORN _____ DIED _____

SIBLING

BORN _____ DIED _____

SIBLING

BORN _____ DIED _____

Family Medical History

Use this page to record hereditary family diseases
such as diabetes, cancer, or heart disease.

Example

Relative   *Aunt Dorothy (Grandmother's Sister)*

Disease   *Diabetes*   Was this cause of death   [X] YES [ ] NO

Diagnosed at age   *59*   Age at Death   *77*

Comments (example)   *Aunt Dorothy was diagnosed early and kept to her exercise
and diet, which helped her live so many more years*

Relative _____

Disease _____   Was this cause of death   [ ] YES [ ] NO

Diagnosed at age _____   Age at Death _____

Comments _____
_____

Relative _____

Disease _____   Was this cause of death   [ ] YES [ ] NO

Diagnosed at age _____   Age at Death _____

Comments _____
_____

Relative _____

Disease _____   Was this cause of death   [ ] YES [ ] NO

Diagnosed at age _____   Age at Death _____

Comments _____

Family Medical History

Use this page to record hereditary family diseases
such as diabetes, cancer, or heart disease.

Relative _____

Disease _____ Was this cause of death ☐ YES ☐ NO

Diagnosed at age _____ Age at Death _____

Comments (example) _____

_____

Relative _____

Disease _____ Was this cause of death ☐ YES ☐ NO

Diagnosed at age _____ Age at Death _____

Comments _____

_____

Relative _____

Disease _____ Was this cause of death ☐ YES ☐ NO

Diagnosed at age _____ Age at Death _____

Comments _____

_____

Relative _____

Disease _____ Was this cause of death ☐ YES ☐ NO

Diagnosed at age _____ Age at Death _____

Comments _____

List the details of any other family health issues, such as allergies, alcoholism, or depression, of which your relatives should be aware.

Location of Family Memorabilia

Some of the previous information in this chapter may have already been compiled in a family Bible, scrapbooks, letters, or other locations. Please use this page to tell relatives where this information can be found and the location of

My Legacy Drawer (See page 145).

Example:

There is a cedar chest in the guest bedroom filled with antiques from Grandmother so please make sure those are carefully unwrapped and given to my brothers. In the closet are 85 photo albums that are the history of our family and of my life. Please give them to the designated family historian.

_____

_____

_____

_____

_____

_____

_____

_____

_____

_____

_____

_____

_____

_____

_____

"Love is how you stay alive,
even after you are gone."

— *Morrie Schwartz*

Chapter 5

Exit Dancing

My Final Arrangements

All our lives we make big plans. We plan for the weather, the weekend, for weddings, for timetables and schedules, meetings and deadlines. We adjust our clocks, adjust the thermostat, adjust our attitudes. We hurry to make it across town, keep appointments, arrive late and leave early. We set the alarm, set the table, and upset each other. Our families help us and hurt us, then help us again. We count our blessings, count our change, and count to ten. We fill the gas tank, fill out forms, fill our wineglass. We make money, we make love, and we make amends. We break the rules and break our word, pick up the pieces and begin again. We pay the bills, pay our dues, and pay the piper. The schedule life holds for most is in and out, up and down, back and forth. Day in and day out, the seconds become minutes; the minutes, hours; the hours pass into weeks, into years, into decades. Suddenly, overnight, we have done what would have taken a lifetime to achieve. We are grown up now—responsible adults. When we look behind us, we see more than when we look ahead. How did the tables turn like this? At what point in the journey did we get closer to the end? We realize, all too slowly, we must prepare for winter in the seasons of our lives. And once again, we must make plans.

It is doubtful you would want to plan

one of life's most momentous occasions within 48 to 72 hours and under intense emotional strain, with little or no idea of cost. Yet, that's exactly what most of us leave our family to do after we die. Rather than peace and resolution for our survivors, funeral arrangements often breed chaos, misgivings, and excessive expense.

Not only will writing down your memorial instructions ensure the service you want, it will also guide your family in such practical matters as type of casket and grave marker, burial instructions, and desired expenditures. In turn, the last remembrances of your presence on earth will evoke memories that bring comfort to loved ones.

"Wherever a beautiful soul has been there
is a trail of beautiful memories."
— *Ronald Reagan*

Don't Cry for Me

Do not stand at my grave and weep;

I am not here, I do not sleep.

I am a thousand winds that blow;

I am the diamond glints on snow.

I am the sunlight on ripened grain;

I am the gentle autumn's rain.

When you awaken in the morning's hush,

I am the swift uplifting rush

of quiet birds in circled flight.

I am the soft star that shines at night.

Do not stand at my grave and cry,

I am not here, I did not die.

—Author Unknown

Funeral/Memorial Arrangements

I would like _____

to be responsible for my funeral/memorial arrangements.

My preferences are as follows:

Funeral Home _____

Burial or Vault

Plot or Vault Location _____

Location of Plot/Vault Deed _____

Type of Vault _____

Type of Casket _____

Casket Color (outside/inside)_____ ☐ Open ☐ Closed

Type of Pall _____

Burial Attire _____

Jewelry _____

Hairstyle Instructions _____

Desired Hairstylist _____ Phone _____

Make-up Instructions _____

Desired Pallbearers

_____

_____

_____

Cremation

Ashes to be Interred at _____

By _____

Type of Urn _____

Disposition of Ashes _____

I would like my funeral/memorial:

☐ Open to all   ☐ Open only to family members and close friends

☐ Organized by my family   ☐ Other _____

I would like my funeral, memorial to be held at:

_____

_____

I would like _____ to conduct the service.

Address _____

Phone _____ email _____

The following is a special poem (you may attach a separate page), scripture or quote that I have always held near and dear to my heart. I would like it to be used in the remembrance card or printed program for my funeral service. (Specify if you want a photograph included in the program.)

_____

_____

_____

_____

_____

I would like the following music to be played at my service
(specify live, recorded, or on mobile devices):

_____

_____

My desire regarding flowers:

_____

_____

_____

I would like the following music, scriptures, poems, etc:

_____

_____

_____

_____

I would like the following people to speak, if willing:

_____

_____

_____

Special comments or requests:
I would like charitable donations in my memory sent to:
Example: I would like donations to go to St. Jude's Hospital

_____

_____

_____

_____

Other Arrangements

Funeral costs increase each year, so what you can afford now may be far less affordable in the future. Contact your insurance agent or preferred funeral home to set up a plan to cover the expenses of your funeral in advance.

[ ] My funeral arrangements have been prepaid with:

_____

If not, the amount I would like to have budgeted for my funeral/memorial arrangements, including casket, is $ _____

[ ] I have   [ ] have not established a fund to cover my funeral expenses with

_____

(Include address and phone number of insurance agent, funeral home, etc.)

_____

_____

_____

_____

Type of Memorial Marker _____

Epitaph, Obituary:

I would like my Obituary Notice to include the following: (I suggest writing this and keeping it updated where it just resides loosely on this page. You may also want to designate a budget.)

_____

_____

_____

I would like my Obituary Notice to be in the following newspapers:

_____

_____

_____

The Voice of Experience

A very close friend sent this letter to me when her mother died.
It punctuates the voice of experience.

Dear Susan,

This subject of death is so hard that I simply decided to write a letter to you telling you what my family and I have gone through.

The first decision that had to be made by me was the "pulling of the plug." Fortunately, Mom had a Durable Power of Attorney for Healthcare and a Living Will. She had stated to her doctor in previous meetings that she did not want life support systems beyond brain death. I think they only put her on the system at noon that day to give me time to get to Oklahoma and make my peace. After nine hours of watching her on that machine, its hideous, constant clanking, I gathered Janet and Rick and said it was time to give her some peace and quiet. Surrounding Mom with ourselves and our love, we watched the doctor remove the abusive tubes and sat with her in silence as she took in her last breath. As heartbreaking as it was, we felt a certain amount of strength because we had made the decision to let her go. That was 5:30 A.M., April 17.

By 9 A.M., the entire family was congregated at Mom's house. My uncles and Mary Ann were trying to make necessary lists for funeral arrangements. We were emotionally distraught, had been up all night, and were novices in this matter anyway. It would have been such a relief to go to a document and learn from Mom's own words just how she wanted her funeral to take place. The idea of one's own choice should play a big part in the funeral. The family has berths at the mausoleum and she was placed next to Dad, so we were spared that decision.

Our next trauma was picking a casket. We went top of the line with Mom and I don't to this day regret it. But once again, it can't be emphasized enough how easy this whole process would be if a document stating everything you want were there to be read. I almost feel it is a person's responsibility to provide guidelines for their own funeral for economic reasons.

Mom was buried on Saturday. We must have spent some portion of the next five days with the lawyers, gathering all of Mom's records for the IRS. The most important fact that I have to say about the decision of selecting an attorney is to establish a fee basis upfront by which he or she will be paid. Don't be afraid to ask and get a concrete answer on that price. You also have to like these people and have a good rapport with them as you will spend a lot of time with them over the next months, or as in our case, years.

It took us all summer and part of the fall to clear Mom's house of her things. I strongly suggest giving this process some time, meaning two or three months, before doing anything. Emotionally, it is draining. But at the same time, don't let too much time pass; it may become impossible to face. We had to prepare Mom's house for sale. Here again is a choice a person can and should make. Possessions should be securely labeled and set aside for people or dealt with in the deceased's own way.

Please bear with me. A lot of this stuff I'm still going through and it is very difficult to write about just now.

Love, Carol

Vital Statistics

(May be required for Death Certificate)

Current Name _____

Name on Birth Certificate _____

Other Names during Your Life _____

Address _____

_____

_____

_____

Phone _____ Cell _____

email _____

Years at Current Address _____

Current Occupation and Title _____

Past Occupations _____

_____

_____

Current Business Address _____

_____

_____

Business Phone _____

Social Security No. _____

Veteran's Serial No. _____

Date of Birth _____ / _____ / _____

Place of Birth _____

(Hospital/Home, City, County, State, Country)

Citizenship _____

Religious Affiliation _____

Spouse's Name _____

Spouse's Birthplace _____

Date and Place of Marriage _____

Father's Complete Name _____

Father's Birthplace _____

Mother's Maiden name _____

Mother's Complete Name _____

Mother's Birthplace _____

Professional Advisors
My trusted professional advisors are listed below for ease of contact.

Executor _____

Address _____

Phone _____ Cell _____

email _____

Trustee of Estate _____

Address _____

Phone _____ Cell _____

email _____

Attorney _____

Address _____

Phone _____ Cell _____

email _____

Financial Advisor _____

Address _____

Phone _____ Cell _____

email _____

Tax Advisor _____

Address _____

Phone _____ Cell _____

email _____

My preference for who should go through my personal belongings:

Name _____ Relationship _____

Phone _____ Cell _____

email _____

email Safe Combination _____

Keys location _____

Special Request(s) _____

My preference for who should go through my files/computer at home:

Name _____ Relationship _____

Phone _____ Cell _____

email _____

User Name/Password _____

My preference for who should go through my files/computer at the office:

Name _____ Relationship _____

Phone _____ Cell _____

email _____

User Name/Password _____

My preference for who should go through my safe deposit box:

Name _____ Relationship _____

Phone _____ Cell _____

email _____

User Name/Password _____

It is helpful to print 10-15 Death Certificates from the county to send out to financial institutions, credit card companies, newspapers and others who will request it.

Consider this: All records that involve financial matters should be gone through by one person and the executor or trustee. Access to your safe deposit box requires one to be named on the signature card. After your death, your executor may also have access, but he or she will need proof of your death and his or her executorship.

For Your Information

In the event of my death, I would like to have:

Name _____

Phone _____ Cell _____

email _____

Additionally, I would like to have:

Name _____

Phone _____ Cell _____

email _____

Contact the following relatives, close friends and neighbors

Name _____

Phone _____ Cell _____

email _____

Name _____

Phone _____ Cell _____

email _____

Name _____

Phone _____ Cell _____

email _____

Name _____

Phone _____ Cell _____

email _____

Others to contact

Religious Leader(s) _____ Phone _____

_____ Phone _____

_____ Phone _____

_____ Phone _____

Physicians _____ Phone _____

_____ Phone _____

_____ Phone _____

Dentist _____ Phone _____

Employer _____ Phone _____

Co-workers _____ Phone _____

_____ Phone _____

_____ Phone _____

_____ Phone _____

Others _____ Phone _____

_____ Phone _____

_____ Phone _____

_____ Phone _____

_____ Phone _____

_____ Phone _____

Others to be contacted may include your housekeeper, gardener, hairdresser, veterinarian, etc.

Professional Societies/Organizations to Contact

Society/Organization _____

Contact _____

Phone _____ Cell _____

email _____

Society/Organization _____

Contact _____

Phone _____ Cell _____

email _____

Volunteer Affiliations to Contact

Affiliation _____

Contact _____

Phone _____ Cell _____

email _____

Affiliation _____

Contact _____

Phone _____ Cell _____

email _____

Affiliation _____

Contact _____

Phone _____ Cell _____

email _____

Personal Notes

List important things to remember for this chapter and check them off one by one.

Chapter 6

Practical Issues

Getting Organized

I need to get organized, I think to myself. Behind hat boxes and shoe boxes, last year's styles, and tomorrow's dry cleaning, I reach into the darkness of my closet. The jewelry box has seen better days, its hinges worn and mirror broken. Inside, treasures lay wrapped in tissue. A dance card from junior high, its tiny pencil dangling from twisted string, a lonely heart wallflower left unattended. A letter from World War II includes a snapshot of some distant cousin twice removed. A broken necklace, a pressed pansy, a marriage license from 1894. I need to get organized, I think to myself. The same thought has crossed my mind for years, each time I have moved this jewelry box and its precious cargo. The contents reflect a simpler time, when a man's word and his handshake were all that was needed, where people called each other neighbor, and left their doors unlocked at night. This is not the case now. Life is complicated, all plastic cards and magnetic strips, digital display, secret codes, changes and button-pushing, email, Facebook, texting, passwords, Twitter and other social media platforms have put extra pressures on all of us for sure. I need to consider the practical issues of bank accounts, insurance policies and estate planning. My mind wanders as I slip onto my finger the soft gold band my father gave my mother. I need to get organized, I think to myself. I need to consider the practical issues.

Getting organized comes easier for some than others.

This chapter contains answers to common questions regarding your estate, making a Will, choosing an executor, and other considerations that will simplify the burden of decision making for your family. Included are examples of a Living Will and organ donor forms, as well as valuable information concerning Social Security and Veterans' benefits.

Ease the trauma of your loved ones by clearly guiding them to the pertinent information they will need. On the following pages, identify the location or a trusted confidant who knows the location of important documents, bank accounts, passwords, insurance policies, deeds, and records.

"No time on earth is long enough to share with those we love or to prepare our hearts for that last good-bye."
— *Alarie Tennile*

So what is **My Legacy Drawer?** It is an easy-to-get-to drawer some place in your home that holds all pertinent documents that are needed for your executor and family in the event you are not able to handle your affairs. This is a crucial must do to make it easy for them to get to it quickly and know what it is.

Record of Important Documents, Etc.

My Legacy Drawer

For added security, after you have filled this out, you may want to copy this page and place it in an envelope to be in your file labeled Personal Information. Passwords are ever changing. This is another page that could be cut out and be kept up to date.

Document Location/Trusted Confidant(s)

Certificates

Birth _____

Adoption _____

Citizenship Papers _____

Marriage _____

Social Security Card _____

Ready Cash for Spouse _____

Will _____

Trust Agreements _____

Guardian Records for Minors _____

_____

Living Will _____

Organ Donor Card _____

Power of Attorney Agreement _____

Military Service Records _____

Military Discharge Papers _____

Medical Records _____

_____

_____

_____

Disability Claims _____

_____

Diplomas _____

_____

My Legacy Drawer Guide

Location of your My Legacy Drawer _____

Contents Guide

My Legacy Drawer should be organized with your important documents and have all the necessary files clearly marked. I suggest doing it alphabetically to make it easier to navigate.

Below is a list of what can be in that drawer among other treasured pictures, etc. This is a good thing to have if there is a need to get out of your home quickly, as this will be one of the first things to pack.

1. **The book** – My Living Legacy can reside right in the front of the drawer when it is not at your bedside table for easy use when you feel like writing in it. It holds all of the information a person will need to know handwritten in your own writing with your special wishes. For confidentiality, these letters that are written in the book can be cut out and placed in envelopes for loved ones. You may choose to make a file for these letters and place them inside your Personal Letters folder. You may also want to add pictures.

2. **Your Will and Estate Plans** with your Executor and Power of Attorney's names and how to contact them for your family.

3. **Financial Records** with details and locations of accounts at banks and other institutions.

4. **Budget of Monthly Expenses** and where they are located on your computer with password if it is in QuickBooks or some other platform.

5. **Insurance Policies** with Health, Auto, Disability, Life Insurance and a cover letter explaining all additional information needed.

6. **Tax Returns** for the past 7 years if by some strange reason you may be audited by the IRS and, of course, for your records to all be together for your Executor.

7. **Passwords** typed out on a word document so that it can be changed periodically. Make sure you keep it updated and dated.

8. **Personal Documents** like birth certificates, deeds, social security card, etc. Perhaps copies of your cards.

9. **Safe-Deposit Box Key**. Location and who has access to it i.e., Executor, Spouse or other person.

10. **Funeral Plans** which are also in this book with your special wishes and documents regarding where and what you would like to do.

11. **Genealogy of your family** if it has been created along with special letters, pictures and more that could be passed down to your family and loved ones that you received or wrote yourself and want to share. Please make sure you write down where your scrapbooks can be found in this file.

Document Location/Trusted Confidant(s)

Retirement/Pension Records _____

_____

Investment Records _____

_____

Debt Records _____

_____

Active Credit Cards _____

_____

Bank Records _____

_____

Safe-Deposit Box _____

_____

Income Tax Returns _____

_____

Real Property Deeds _____

_____

Titles (Cars, Boats, Etc.) _____

_____

Business Agreements _____

_____

Nuptial Agreements _____

_____

Divorce Decree _____

Other Location/Trusted Confidant(s)

Photo copy credit cards with security numbers to place in this document

Safe-Deposit Box Key _____

Safe Combination _____

Home Keys _____

Car Keys _____

File Keys _____

Extra Keys _____

Security PIN Numbers _____

_____

Combination Lock Numbers _____

Computer Information _____

User Name _____

Passwords for computer, smart phone and other devices: _____

_____

_____

_____

Manuals _____

Warranties/Insurance _____

Special Operation Instructions _____

_____

Other Miscellaneous items _____

_____

For added assurance, have extra copies of important documents accessible to one or more trusted confidant(s). Keep these copies in a safe place in your home (My Legacy Drawer), a fireproof box, plus store a copy in your safe-deposit box or with your Executor.

Insurance Records

Life Insurance

Company _____ Beneficiary _____

Location of Policy _____

Company _____ Beneficiary _____

Location of Policy _____

Company _____ Beneficiary _____

Location of Policy _____

Pensions/Annuities

Company _____ Beneficiary _____

Location of Contract _____

Company _____ Beneficiary _____

Location of Contract _____

Company _____ Beneficiary _____

Location of Contract _____

Other

Company/Type _____

Location _____

Company/Type _____

Location _____

Other Items/Documents

Item or Document _____

Location _____

Item or Document _____

Location _____

Item or Document _____

Location _____

Item or Document _____

Location _____

Item or Document _____

Location _____

Item or Document _____

Location _____

Item or Document _____

Location _____

Item or Document _____

Location _____

Item or Document _____

Location _____

Item or Document _____

Location _____

Item or Document _____

Location _____

A special friend who lost her sister wanted to share her experience.

Susan,

You need to identify who is responsible for filing insurance claims. If someone has been ill for a long time with institutional care, the unfiled claims could go back for years. My sister was just too ill to file claims for as far back as two years. She paid thousands for medicines that were not claimed on her insurance. She also had tests and procedures for which I filed claims that paid thousands to us.

Often people have cancer policies that do not pay an institution but pay directly to the insured. Therefore, no institution will file for you. I was unaware that my sister had such a policy, but after finding some papers, I investigated and filed them, which in my sister's case resulted in a significant payment to her estate.

I consider insurance a very big issue as it is very time-consuming and confusing. I spent about three months locating items, getting proper documentation, and filing claims. Also, it can be one of the most valuable gifts you leave in your estate.

Vivian

This diagram is to help you get started in identifying the types of insurance policies you may have.

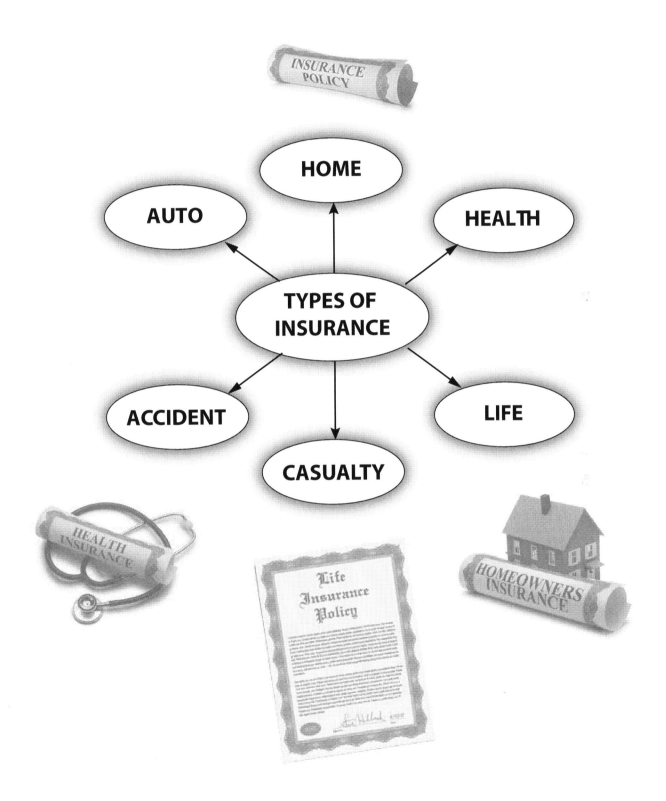

Your Will

A Will is a plan for your financial affairs after you depart, but it also brings peace of mind while you are living. It is a document that explains what will happen to the things you own, who will care for your minor children, and who will serve as executor to settle your affairs. It is your guarantee that important decisions you made in your lifetime will be carried out according to your wishes.

What will happen if you don't have a Will?

Laws can vary from state to state, but one thing is guaranteed: someone else will decide how to distribute your estate. Only relatives are allowed to inherit if you die without a Will. This means your friends, former spouse, or favorite charity would receive nothing. If there are no living relatives, it can all be passed to the state. If you have a fiancé(e) or close friend, they will receive nothing.

What is an estate?

Anything you own constitutes your estate. That includes bank accounts, stocks, cars, jewelry, real estate, businesses, coin collections, or art collections. Your Will determines what specific items will be left to certain individuals.

Wills seldom deal with the distribution of personal belongings as addressed in this workbook. Accordingly, the information herein is an informal supplement to your Will. In any event, sharing this workbook with your Will originator, your Executor, or a trusted confidant will help communicate your full intentions.

What property is not covered by a Will?

Specific types of property are not covered by a Will:

· Life insurance and retirement plans that designate individuals or any entity other than the deceased's estate as the beneficiary are not covered by a Will.

· Property you have placed in a Living Trust during your lifetime goes to the trust's beneficiaries.

· Property you have owned as a joint tenant will automatically be inherited by the co-owner(s).

In certain states, the money, real estate, and possessions you and your spouse acquire during your marriage are considered community property. If one spouse earns more than another, the property is still equal in distribution. Your Will can affect only your half of the community property.

Be sure your Will is kept current and that your Executor or confidant knows its location.

I suggest creating a **My Legacy Drawer** (See page 145) that has all of the necessary documents and this book for family members to easily find. This is critical.

Your Executor

When selecting an executor, it is most important to remember that the person you leave in charge of your affairs can no longer turn to you for advice, leaving the decisions regarding your estate totally in his or her hands. Many of these questions are simply matters of taste or preference, while others require expert knowledge of tax law. An appropriate executor is a person who is totally trustworthy and knows your beneficiaries. For every beneficiary there will be a different point of view as to your intentions.

The attitude "I'll be long gone, let someone else worry about who gets what" is very shortsighted when talking about those who love you. A perfect example is the husband who has always taken full financial responsibility for his family. The wife receives an allowance for household needs, without any worry as to from where the money comes. When the husband dies suddenly, she is made the executor of the estate. This can be an overwhelming task to someone who has never had to balance a checkbook. Make a conscientious choice. Do not ask more of your loved ones after your death than you would have in life.

Periodically, be sure to take your executor and main beneficiary through your home, pointing out personal belongings with special memories and intentions. Sharing this book with them before you die will be the closest you get to being at the reading of your own Will. Help them out. Be their guide through this ordeal. It will lighten their emotional burden, and you can rest peacefully knowing your wishes will be accomplished.

Your Living Will

If you desire to entrust your life's wishes to a loved one in the event you become totally disabled, you need a Living Will.

Following is an example of a Living Will:

Living Will

To my family, physician, lawyer, and clergy:

To any medical facility in whose care I happen to be:

To any individual who may become responsible for my health, welfare, or affairs:

I wish to make this statement as an expression of my desires while I am still of sound and competent mind. If a time comes when I can no longer take part in decisions regarding my own well-being, let this statement serve as a guide to all those who care for me.

Should a situation arise when there is no reasonable expectation of my recovering from extreme physical or mental disability, I request that I be allowed to die and not be kept alive by artificial means or "heroic measures" undertaken by medical personnel. I do, however, ask that medication be mercifully administered to me to alleviate pain and suffering even though this may hasten the moment of death.

If I have executed a valid form of bequeathal of any of my organs for transplant or research purposes, I do ask and authorize that I be kept alive by artificial means for a time sufficient to enable the medical personnel to accomplish the withdrawal of the organs.

I am making this request after careful consideration and it is in accordance with my beliefs and convictions. I hope that those who care for me will feel morally bound to carry out my wishes as expressed here.

Signature _____ Date _____

Witness _____

Witness _____

Living Wills are different from state to state. A letter from you will not be honored by law. Overall, a Living Will states that if there is no hope and your death is imminent, you do not wish to be kept alive by artificial means. You must use the form from your own state.

Organ Donation

Donation of your body or specific organs should not be a part of your Will for the simple reason that it's often discovered too late to honor your wishes. Make sure your doctor and your family have copies of the appropriate form.

Following is an example of a Uniform Donor Card:

A Uniform Donor Card

of _____
(Print or type name of donor)

In the hope that I may help others, I hereby make this anatomical gift, if medically acceptable, to take effect upon my death. The words and marks below indicate my desires.

I give: (a) any needed or physical parts.

           (b) only the following organs or physical parts:

              _____
                  (specify organs or physical parts)
           for the purpose of transplantation, therapy, medical research or education.

           (c) my body for anatomical study if needed.

Limitations or special wishes, if any:

Signed by the donor and the following two witnesses in the presence of each other:

Signature of donor _____Birthdate of donor _____

Date signed _____   City and State _____

Witness _____   Witness _____

Similar to Living Wills, Organ Donor forms vary from state to state. You must use the form from your own state.

Social Security Benefits

Social Security is a form of insurance that should be attended to after any death. Most of us are entitled to some form of these benefits. But it is important to realize that Social Security benefits are not paid automatically. One must apply for these benefits on special forms, and certain documents must be furnished at that time. The forms and documents listed below must be furnished within a specific time limit.

- Certified Copy of Death Certificate
- Social Security Card or Number
- Copy of Marriage Certificate
- Birth Certificate of Applicant
- Birth Certificate of Deceased
- Birth Certificates of Minor Children
- Disability Proof for Children over 18
- Receipted Funeral Bill
  (If applicant is other than the surviving spouse)
- Proof of Support if Applicant is Parent or Husband

As appropriate, designate the location of these documents in the earlier section of this chapter. You may wish to asterisk the documents relevant to obtaining Social Security benefits for your family.

Contact your local Social Security Office for current information on benefits and claims procedures, at (800) 772-1213 or visit the website: **www.ssa.gov**

Veterans' Benefits

Survivors of veterans are entitled to many burial-related benefits. However, these benefits will not be paid automatically. Claims for Veterans' benefits must be made within certain prescribed time limits.

As an honorably discharged veteran from the Air Force, Army, Navy, Marine Corps, or Coast Guard, you may be entitled to the following:

- A burial allowance for expenses can be found on **www.va.gov.** This allowance will be paid only for veterans who were entitled to receive a Veterans Administration pension or compensation.

- A limited allowance for burial and funeral expenses of the deceased.

- A burial flag, that can be given to the next of kin or friend of the deceased.

- A bronze memorial or granite grave marker.

To have your claim filed, the following forms may be required:

- Veteran's Discharge Papers
- Certified Copy of Death Certificate
- Copy of Marriage Certificate
- Birth Certificate of Minor Children

As appropriate, designate the location of these documents in the earlier section of this chapter. As with the documents needed for obtaining Social Security benefits, you may wish to asterisk such documents for ease of obtaining family benefits.

Veterans' benefits are frequently altered and revised. There may also be Veterans benefits from your county. To determine your eligibility or to file your claim, contact your local Veterans Affairs office or call (800) 827-1000 or visit the website: **www.va.gov**

Personal Thoughts & Reflections

Use these pages for any additional entries you may wish to include.

"No light that was born in love
can ever be extinguished."

— *Darcie D. Sims, Ph.D.*

Chapter 7

Sands of Time

In the stillness of the night I travel to familiar places in my mind. The grandfather clock ticks a steady heartbeat through the hushed quiet and I am comforted by its sound. Like hearing the footsteps of a parent down a long hallway, I feel safe. I know this clock has seen generations of my family, though where it stands has changed often. Some things do not change: we are born, we learn to rise after falling down, we laugh in the middle of our tears, and we hope love will find us on our journey. Always too soon, it seems, we die. This scenario can be short or long, bittersweet or joy-filled, riddled with angst or iced with excitement, but generally it is like a wave upon the sand, ever lapping at the shore in a rhythm all its own. We can neither start nor stop it, only interrupt it with our presence, and appreciate it while we're there. Like my grandfather clock, my face, too, has grown older, but each hour still chimes, and I realize how grateful I am to have been a particle in the sands of time.

For convenience in contacting loved ones who have received
special thoughts or gifts herein, list their names and addresses below.
You may also paste them in.

Name _____ Relationship _____

Address _____

Phone _____ Cell _____

email _____

Name _____ Relationship _____

Address _____

Phone _____ Cell _____

email _____

Name _____ Relationship _____

Address _____

Phone _____ Cell _____

email _____

Name _____ Relationship _____

Address _____

Phone _____ Cell _____

email _____

Name _____ Relationship _____

Address _____

Phone _____ Cell _____

email _____

Name _____ Relationship _____

Address _____

Phone _____ Cell _____

email _____

Name _____ Relationship _____

Address _____

Phone _____ Cell _____

email _____

Name _____ Relationship _____

Address _____

Phone _____ Cell _____

email _____

Name _____ Relationship _____

Address _____

Phone _____ Cell _____

email _____

Name _____ Relationship _____

Address _____

Phone _____ Cell _____

email _____

Name _____ Relationship _____

Address _____

Phone _____ Cell _____

email _____

Name _____ Relationship _____

Address _____

Phone _____ Cell _____

email _____

Name _____ Relationship _____

Address _____

Phone _____ Cell _____

email _____

Name _____ Relationship _____

Address _____

Phone _____ Cell _____

email _____

Name _____ Relationship _____

Address _____

Phone _____ Cell _____

email _____

Name _____ Relationship _____

Address _____

Phone _____ Cell _____

email _____

Name _____ Relationship _____

Address _____

Phone _____ Cell _____

email _____

Passwords

So much of our daily lives now revolve around passwords. To share with loved ones or a trusted friend or partner, you may record them here, print a copy from your computer and keep in a file drawer, and for safe keeping, print a copy to keep in **My Legacy Drawer** (See page 145). Simply paste the printout on these pages and remember to date changes, include security code logins for computers, phones, tablets and other devices.

URL _____

User Name _____

Password _____

URL _____

User Name _____

Password _____

URL _____

User Name _____

Password _____

URL _____

User Name _____

Password _____

URL _____

User Name _____

Password _____

URL _____

User Name _____

Password _____

Passwords

URL _____

User Name _____

Password _____

URL _____

User Name _____

Password _____

URL _____

User Name _____

Password _____

URL _____

User Name _____

Password _____

URL _____

User Name _____

Password _____

URL _____

User Name _____

Password _____

URL _____

User Name _____

Password _____

URL _____

User Name _____

Password _____

How you can help a loved one complete this book...

Did you know that many families have a historian who is committed to writing down all the information that should be passed down to family members? They say it is every third generation. Are you that person?

All families have gatherings like Thanksgiving, holidays, birthdays and more throughout the year where stories are told — sometimes over and over. But, who writes these stories down and makes them available to a family member? This book offers a way to make that happen. Take this workbook to heart and make sure you document these most incredible moments for all.

Think about interviewing your parents on a monthly basis to gather information and to listen to stories, backgrounds and the legacy of your family. Have this book with you to guide you along the way. It is not just for someone to fill out, it is for family members to ask questions at any age as well. Also, consider filling this book out for a loved one if they are unable to do it themselves. Be sure to write down any information you can obtain for them and ask those important questions. Stories are folklore and magical to pass down.

It is said that the storyteller in the family may not be the writer of the family, however, the historian could take that over and make sure to gather information as it is told, so please find that person if you are not the one and make sure it is captured. This book is a way of sharing your collective identity as a family. When one tells a story, it shapes destinies.

Leave "My Living Legacy" by your bedside to write in at any time. Remember, all this information takes a lifetime to create bust just a few moments to put in writing.

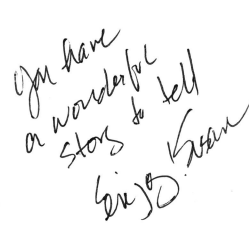

The Susan Fielder Way

In 2013 Pancreatic Cancer took Susan Fielder's much-loved husband Dan Mears. Years earlier her mother, Guynelle passed suddenly and so, too, a little girl, named Jennifer, who was like Susan's own child, lost her battle with Leukemia during that same year. Most would understand if Susan curled up in a ball, wrapped in grief.

But, that is not the Susan Fielder way. Instead, Susan's initial thought was "how can I help other people knowing what I know now."

My Living Legacy is the result.

A musician/song writer, artist, poet, designer, writer, and highly successful businesswoman, Susan is courageous, innovative, creative, energetic and committed. A walk through Susan's world is an exciting journey revealing a passionate woman inspired by art and sustained by her empathy for others.

Susan designed **My Living Legacy** as an easy-to-use guidebook to create a personal journal to guide loved ones in making essential, often difficult, decisions. It is her hope "that the anguish of others will be diminished through the use of this journal."

Susan believes, "If you don't write it down, it won't get passed down."

Susan Fielder is the Founder of Susan Fielder & Associates, Inc., a sales promotion/marketing consultancy in San Diego. She served on the Board of Directors for the UC San Diego Sulpizio Cardiovascular Center, is a past judge for The Finest Service Awards for the San Diego Convention & Visitors Bureau, a graduate of San Diego's LEAD program, past member of the Women Presidents' Organization and a winner of the San Diego Business Journal's Woman of the Year Marketing Award as well as Woman of the Year for the Leukemia Society.

But, all these accomplishments take a back seat to her devotion to supporting the treatment and cure of Pancreatic Cancer, which takes over 50,000 lives a year. Her passion guided her to create a new venture called iPlaid (standing for Intuitive Passion Launches an Inner Discovery).

She invites you to join her on her quest by viewing her websites **www.susanfielderart.com** and **www.iplaid.org** where a portion of all sales go to generate revenue for pancreatic cancer researchers who are on the path to a cure.

Susan welcomes any suggestions and ideas to make a difference.

This book is dedicated to her husband, Dan Mears,
who was called the "King of Grace" and guided Susan to always be the best that she could be.

Corporate Programs:

If you are in the following industries, the book *My Living Legacy* has proven to be an extremely effective tool in building long-term client relationships and enabling you to pass on your services from generation to generation.

- Insurance Industry
- Death Care Market
- Fundraising
- Planned Giving for Foundations
- Trust Departments
- Financial Planning
- Attorneys

In addition, *My Living Legacy* is a memorable, practical and heart-warming gift item that is appropriate for all occasions.

Susan Fielder is an author, businesswoman, entrepreneur, entertainer, fund-raiser, and artist in the San Diego area.

To contact Susan: susan@susanfielder.com *or* info@mylivinglegacy.life
858-395-8466

Customization and volume discounts available. Please call for information.

Your advice please...

To help others prepare their living legacies in the best and most thoughtful way, I would love to hear your suggestions or comments.

Please visit **www.MyLivingLegacy.life** and complete the online **Advice Please Form**. If you would be so kind, please take a moment to share your insights, feelings and stories of how this book impacted your family. Please share this book with friends and family so they too can feel the power of **My Living Legacy**. It is a gift to see the hand written words of a loved one as well as their genuine thoughts articulated by their well known style of penmanship. This is an each-one reach-one opportunity to give this legacy gift to others.

I look forward to your stories.

Blessings,

Susan Fielder

To order additional copies of *My Living Legacy,*
visit: **www.amazon.com** or **www.MyLivingLegacy.life**

Made in the USA
Columbia, SC
08 November 2021